AVAILABLE LIGHT

Maria McManus

/...the stilling of one heart, quickening the other.../

AVAILABLE LIGHT

ARLEN HOUSE

Available Light

is published in 2018 by
ARLEN HOUSE
42 Grange Abbey Road
Baldoyle, Dublin 13, Ireland
Phone: 00 353 85 7695597
arlenhouse@gmail.com
arlenhouse.blogspot.com

Distributed internationally by
SYRACUSE UNIVERSITY PRESS
621 Skytop Road, Suite 110
Syracuse, NY 13244–5290
Phone: 315–443–5534
Fax: 315–443–5545
supress@syr.edu
syracuseuniversitypress.syr.edu

978–1–85132–187–2, *paperback*
978–1–85132–188–9, *limited edition, signed and numbered hardback*

front cover image by Helen Bradbury
back cover image by Deirdre McKenna

LOTTERY FUNDED

Contents

for MJ

Available Light

INTRODUCTION

> Who does not know that this city was founded only after taking the auspices, that everything in war and in peace, at home and abroad was done only after taking the auspices
>
> – Livy, Roman historian, born 64/59BC

The role of Augurs in ancient times was to observe four quadrants of the sky, drawing conclusions from both the flight paths (*alites*) and vocalisations (*oscines*) of the birds. Augurs were the conduits and interpreters of the *impetrativa* (requests from the people to the gods) and *oblativa* (messages sent from the gods to the people). While augural law was rigorously secret, valid signals were sought from a hierarchy of birds such as ravens, vultures, eagles, owls and woodpeckers.

This collection of poems was written in the context of an Artist's Career Enhancement Award (ACES) from the Arts Council of Northern Ireland in 2015/16. My intention was to write poems to probe and explore contemporary questions and dilemmas. It was also my intention to experiment with other ways of putting literature into public spaces, which augment the conventions of publishing and public readings. As part of the writing process, and taking a stance that artists are, in a way, augurs, I was intentional in actively engaging with artists from other disciplines. As the poems were written, they were shared and the resultant responses, a soundscape, paintings, photographs and a short documentary film, were exhibited in Down Arts Centre (Downpatrick), Framewerk (Belfast) and The Higher Bridges Gallery (Enniskillen). Further, a collaboration between myself and choreographer Eileen McClory has resulted in a performance of *Dust* (Section III) at The Playhouse (Derry), in a performance developed with the students of Contemporary Dance at the University of Ulster (Magee).

I

Impetrativa

Remnant Nomenclature

1

First, starlings

in dark ballet –
bold scrim across the blue hour
at Albert Bridge,
and the day yielding
into something altogether
more sultry, unknown.

2

You said, *'Like iron filings and a lodestone',*

suddenly, we are liminal

here, now, hovering between Catalina Blue heavens
and back then: a memory measured in luminosity –

adolescents,
school skirts hitched and rolled at the waistband
bare-leggéd, absorbed, conducting experiments

in polarities   and magnetism.

3

In Italy, they say the ravens and the crows speak Latin.

So the answer, in that case,
to any big dilemma, say
for example: *Should I stay? Should I go?*
... when it's worth the opinions of a congress of corvids,

and for times when what you need more than anything
is the perspective only a bird's-eye view delivers –
with due consideration and without unkindness,
the answer will be, the answer will *always* be,

Cras. Cras.[1]

Tomorrow. Tomorrow.

1 *Cras:* the Latin for tomorrow

4

'And the stars of the sky, fell to the earth'.[1]

They are earthed now,
a rabble of shawlies
mocking each other
grubbing amongst the windfalls,

plucky,

on stout pinkish legs –

they have no better sense
than to announce themselves,
draw the wrong attention.

1 from *Stalker*, dir. Andrei Tarkovsky

5

'A Hawk can't be tamed. It's wild and it's fierce.
It's not bothered about anybody'.[1]

Starling's Law falls; the hawk a hitman;
and there it is,
Argo Navis among the Bramleys,
a feathery galaxy pluming
downwind, across the orchard's floor.

The stilling of one heart,
quickening of the other.

1 Character of Billy Casper, in the film *Kes,* dir. Ken Loach

6

Though its prey was pinioned, supine,
the hawk at times lost balance –
a Billy Bunter on a wobble board, watching
its back, looking to see who might be looking.

The starling made a feisty racket in the ambush,
it showed up with gutsy martyrdom – fought the fight
of somebody with nothing left to lose:
all screeching maw,
stabbing, nipping, spearing the hawk's heart.
Its tarsals clutched hard,
grounding the marauder by the anklet,
screaming all the while to be let go,
though it held on fast
as if its own life
depended on it.

7

We all do that, sooner or later,
hold on tight, stay, and keep ourselves
in the line of fire, when going
would be life itself, however uncertain.

It is better then, to make a friend of death,
to let it come, to give in,
than suffer the small deaths
of weak and callous love:
Be soft. Offer no resistance.
Become something all the more elemental.

Give in. Pain is temporal,
and then it's over.

8

Reset the compass.
Salvage tail feathers and wings,
leave all other bones, the body,
the carcass, the unseeing eyes.
Make of your self
a stern, a sail, a hull.

Drop a plumb-line.

Avoid dry land.

A Nightingale

i.m. Marie Wilson

/ … to think of you –
the delicate cathedral of your body;
your life a flyleaf
in a dense November hymnal of histories;

grim confetti

on a broad church;
an island town,
half-remembering.

HEDGEROW

Sotto voce
she sings,
and muted underfoot,
brogues
keep fair, reverent clip
down the country roads,
cortege after cortege.

Among the border farms,
along the country lanes
and bog roads;
banshees
on a roster,
never off the batter.

Faolán. Lupo. Wolf.

1

Have the sea as your wilderness if you must.
I'll take the mountains. I'll take the forest.
I'll take the dark. Give me winter.

The coast can wear a scattering of streetlights
for a necklace in the night
across her black and sensuous skin,
her face hidden from sight.

Bring on the moon –
we will call long into the darkness,
to gather, raise alarm, find one another.

2

I faced death first. Remember that.
If you want the gospel truth, look no further.
Mere marginalia: a hyphen, gall's tattoo,
lapis lazuli, holly. It's all there, lit up
in gorse, wode, ultramarine, orpiment.

Ask the scribes if you really want to know.
They'll tell you everything –
that book is lavish and extravagant.
It wasn't plundered; there is refuge in the library,
it's all lush among the vellum quires of Kells;

In principio erat verbum.
See here, the story of how Ishtar took the hump,
and she sent me among the sheep
as punishment (a woman scorned –
you know the story).

3

Listen up; there are no false prophets;
there is no crying.
We were warned off and away from the doors;
if you must know the turf
was marked in scat all right, but the borders
of ourselves were huge, rangey, far-flung.

Here's the truth.
We only took what was necessary – nothing more.
We made good our share of spoil –
ask the raven, the crow,
the wily magpie, those rare
so-sacred eagles.

They all took our message
to the god of the sky, to the sun,
but what of it? Who among the salmon
took our chronicles to sea?

There's nothing to show for it now.

4

We are of the earth;
make no mistake of that.

We were left to it. So be it.

After Cromwell
wheedled open the miserable
teeming throat of his purse,
head for head
we were just raw bounty.

Six quid the She in whelp. A fiver each, per Duke;
Three pounds a Juvenile.

The hungry, the poor, the biddable-desperate,
left pelt on pelt, hollow, skull-less,
at the docks and slung them on ships
bound for Bristol.

5

The starving make Omérta; we know that.
I could say, we understand, that we know
the way of it. Who could blame them?

Take this scenario;
Your own child is raising hell,
so you hunker, latching its screaming maw
from one mean and scrawny breast to the other,
suckling, but nothing sates the excoriating hunger in it.

Nothing cuts to your own marrow quicker –
it sticks in your craw,
raising your hackles in the pinch,
routing every feral sinew, nerve,
raw instinct.

The sight of your own infant
changed to near-carrion
before your very eyes is enough …

Let me ask you, what would you do?

Anything becomes fair game then.
Besides, I have it on good authority,

once the hunt commences
something will be found.

6

The same old spiel repeats itself.
Don't blame me for skulking
round your door in the night.
These are hungry times.
The stakes are at their highest.
Those that have – let them be the ones
to beg for the viaticum; let's see if that miserly
morsel is enough sustenance then.

As we cross the river I say,
put your red coat on;
drive their cattle to a stampede –
trample them if necessary,
offer wine to all their wives,
have them broach the meniscus
of an everlasting cup –
that will make them docile; ask Bacchus
if you don't believe me.

7

How might I speak with you then?
Will you listen out for me?

Don't mistake my invisibility for absence,
nor my silence either.

I am with you when you are grieving,
when the pounding of your own heart
batters the cavity behind your ribs
and forces the sea though your hearing.

You will remember me
as I pass by. I do not weep
walking the ploughshare.

I am with you when you are grieving.

I beat the path.
I cleared the way.

I faced death first.

The House that Stood for Happiness

1

Where among these feathered paths is rest?
Where the sweet spot,
in half-light, dappled, flickering,
green and airy,
is that sure instinct?
How can we know at last
the place called home?

The blackbird fled her shelter:
her confidence, her trust
in the world came to nothing in the end.
The nest she fashioned, pressed out
with urgent tender heartbeats,
lies abandoned.

The setting bird took flight,
her memories, dreams
of the home of 'then'.

2

I palmed her cold blue eggs,
her latent intimacy:
here, a childhood unlived,
here, a childhood lost.

3

This nest offers its mouth
to the sky. Blades of grass
imprinting against the limits,
fresh as linen. The house
that stood for happiness was lost –
but the heart beats on
for that which curves
and holds,

returning its call,
its sound.

4

Where there is light,
I want *this* place –
between heaven and earth,
a high place for dreaming,
a marriage of moss and down
cupped just out of reach,
given form from my breast,
pressed out with my body,
a dress to fit,
breathed into.

I made good
these un-helpable
palpitations – I put them to work,
searching out the place that knows
the choreography of forest-love,
where the world and its hostilities
are muffled, suffocating, far away –
beyond the trees' cordoning
I have found a place
                                        to sing.

On Falling

Young US pilot, Joe Kittinger, became the first human being to jump to earth from an altitude of 31,300 metres (102,800 feet) – the stratosphere. In the first 4k he reached Mach 0.9 (90% of the speed of sound, 614 mph)

– Stewart & Lynch

1

[Zugunruhe]

Like a starling fledgling
in a cage, in a lab, in a bunker somewhere,
do you know now,
to the marrow of your bones,
an itchy, antsy agitation,
that perch-hopping fever,
that desire to be gone
into the unknown?

2

[Flight]

Have you ever launched a bird back into the air
from your hands, watched its shadow
fade, felt it kick back
upon your palms as it rushed up
spreading its wings,
as it scoffed at gravity?
Were you humbled, envious?

3

[The Bends]

Were you dispensable,
buccaneer, cavalier, mortal,
flirting with life
in a game of chance somewhere
between heroics and self-loathing?
Did you think of Icarus,
hear death calling,
was there one square inch of silence?

4

[Frontiers]

Talk to me about the weather.
Was there trouble in the heavens?
Was the light in tatters?
If, instead, you'd crossed the Kármán line
what then? Meteor? Aurora?
Was earth beautiful but irrelevant.
In the thin nothingness of air,
could you doubt the collusion of gravity?

5

[A Step]

Was there a moment
when you thought
you might never wear out
another pair of shoes
or put your cheek
to the earth?

6

[Earthbound]

Who kept vigil?
Who waited?
Did your mother know
what you were up to?
Who did not dare
lift their eyes
and look skyward?
Whose heart pounded
holding out for news?

7

[Gravity]

And,
when a lover's body
replied, soft and yielding
to your own,
did you let yourself
fall then?

II

Oblativa

LOST

Shroud all your mirrors.
Use the linen that you keep
for good, the silk scarves from India,
the black lace mantillas for which
we have no other use these days.
Put a small light on every ledge,
open the windows and listen
for the neighbour's dog to howl.

Believe that these farewells are necessary;
listen closely for their most intimate
whisperings and let it be enough now.
Release them. They need their time to wander,
free, aimless, over the cartilage
of some broken and abandoned boat,
pilgrim stones, weeds, the unwanted.

You have no right to hold them here,
nor invoke them, nor interrupt their leaving.

                    Instead,
scan the sky   for swallows,

never mind that it's too early in the season –

                    keep looking.

Any day now

                    They will come.
                    They will come.
                    They will come.

Corncrakes

1

Not one among the rushes,
none in the meadows,
none where the farmer dropped to his knees
lamenting the crumpled nest its requiem,
wringing his hands
like a chaplain
bringing bad news
to the door
in the night-time.

Them's rare wee things,
them's rare.

2

… and rarer still,
the small clutch
a universe among the rushes –
small planets grounded in troubled heavens.

These scraplings
scurry in frantic sorties
to grub the undergrowth
amongst the brackens.

It is the night,
it is the stars
impress.

Africa. Africa. Africa.

3

Opening the night,
terra incognita –
there is no map,
only opening the night …
Listen; first intently,
closely – no further than at arms length
and then, when everything is detailed,
clocked and inventoried, and only then,
double the circle.

Listen. Double the circle. Listen.

4

Sense unreachable places,

chance positions,
calm places at the eye
of hurricanes.

Flee your fever
and with unholy impetus
hurl off into the nomadic sky,
into severe places
into unbreachable theatres,

into mystery, uncertainty, doubt,
into ablation,

and tell everything,
when you return.

Peregrinations

1

If you took a chance
and let those plates stop spinning,
stuck your hands in your pockets
or your fingers in your ears
and stepped back –
what would happen then?

After all that clatter
and when the shreds,
all the broken pieces
are shovelled up,
wrapped away carefully
and left somewhere for landfill,
what then?

All that falling can only happen once
and then it's over.

There's an alternative:
you could gather in those plates,
stack them neatly, one on top of the other,
file under *something for someone else*
another time and let them sit there.

Or you could just watch the wobbly poles
come to their inevitable standstill – decide
to let them break, so that
puts a stop to this forever.

One way or another – you could choose
silence, choose stillness, stop playing.

You choose.

2

When Nuria tells me
the Robin died
because it flew into the glass
I know it is true.

It thought
that what it saw
was endless sky –
that this reflection of sky
and the Bay of Biscay was reality.

Its neck had broken
and it lay supine on the steps.
I dare say
death was instant –
I hope so, and that it didn't suffer.

3

I know this one
and will share with you
two stories of my own –
near-misses, if you like.

The first was a dream
of the hummingbird
in all its shimmering brilliance, battering
on the window of my smallest, most under-used room.
Outside I'd made a garden full of colours.
Into it I planted tame versions of my dreams
underneath the wild flowers
that greeted everyone who beat their path
to my front door,

but it was the illusion of the garden
brought the hummingbird
to beat itself to death upon the glass.

4

The second is the story of an interview.
I faced a four-strong panel. They were back-lit
with the afternoon sun
and the scene outside was rich and wonderful –
a river tumbled down a small green glen, all ferns
and damp and luscious. The sounds of water
broke through the stultifying must inside.

I wore funereal black –
considered smart and fitting
for such occasions; an indication
I was serious, reverential,
intentional about the task –
a tailored form of knee-
bending and formality,
a message that I would
conform, concede, submit,
toe-the-line, fit in.

I gathered
my first breath to lift
the register of my voice,
as a summer swallow flew
full tilt into the image
of that garden paradise
and was lost,
as it slammed hard against the glass
and fell into Montbretia.

5

At *The Gower* when we walked
we looked skywards. You could
tell the difference between swifts
and swallows, house-martins and sand-martins.

They're all beautiful to me.
I find that I am mesmerised and gaze
always into the blue of where they are –
and it's enough.

6

Was it you I told the story of the hummingbird to?

I heard Attenborough
talk about them on the radio – of how,
amidst the chaos of this world, and the catastrophic,
devastation of our earth,
there is one small hopeful story, and it is this –

how people have laid a corridor of sweetness
all the way from Costa Rica to the north of North America
and how in this symbiosis
the hummingbirds flourish against all odds –
how they reward the wilderness
of our grey lives,
gem-like and shimmering,
captivating the available light
and give it back to us
as they migrate
North – South – North – South-
North …

so delicate, so tiny
in the dying of this light.

7

And then there is another story –
in the poem of Sah-Sin. Tess Gallagher tells us
it is the Native American name for hummingbird
and she tells how when she found one,
in torpor, in the cold – she lifted it
and slipped it in under her breast
next to her heart, to warm it,
in the hope it would revive again.

8

Here's my last message
to you, for now.

I found a montage
of hummingbirds with the mirror in the mirror,

and I'll play that for you sometime, but –

between here and there
between now and then

don't fear anything.

And if you decide
to stop catching those spinning, falling plates

and if you need something for your hands to hold –
here's mine.

You might.

And if you take a chance,
just think –

then maybe, just maybe,
we could dance again.

Émigrés

1

You might say
these are the words
of some mad-woman,
a pirate queen –
a bandit and a renegade,
but let's talk instead
about the end of time.

Examine this
as if it were a crime scene
and tell the story whole –

This and this alone
will realign the stars
when times are lean.

2

Caged birds mimic the wild;
their sad, lonesome grace notes
betray the longings
of their own small, full hearts.
They make the best of things,
but watch, always,
should a moment come,
the clasp slips,
a gap appears –
for in that instant
they will cast a bigger, fleeting shadow
and spill outwards.

The transgressive
and the sacred share tenancy,
cheek by jowl.

3

What is going on in your heart?

Prisoners of war live here.

Throw off your gaudy vestments,
spring's best and brightest fig
and let me see you naked
and then, more naked still –

Put your heart,
in my heart's cavity.
Slip it in.

Bring your worry beads if needs be.
It's not too late
to shred all documents
of denunciation.

4

Among the missing
those who are gone, unspoken of, delicate murmurings
that could not be spoken
in convent grounds
or beyond a chapel door.

Can we be forgiven
our self-absorption?

The lost raise an echo
in the quiet.

Passive waiting fails.

5

Now we must
hunt by ear and
put our trust

in gossiping swallows,
the hooded crows, the herring gulls,

the wryneck's potent drum.

6

There are strange wailings
on the sea, raucous cries,
sounds on wings,
sounds with wings,
weed and sand,

waves on rock

small, intimate murmurings

valleys of singing birds *the singing, singing birds*

7

Between silences
take notice
of the imago
of your stolen self.

Sold back
but at what price?

8

We fail when we marry
our truth to mediocrity
and parade life's ledgers
balanced without scrutiny.

9

I remember
the smell of bread,
of funeral lilies.

Vivid prayers,
offerings, a darkness,

halos of small flames,
mistakes, intentions.

Lamentations.

10

Collect wishbones,
place them in charnel houses,
quarter the ground
to make sure and certain
none are missing –
these things bring a plan to grief.

11

The song-birds are drowning,
the sea is now a cemetery.

The song-birds are drowning,
the sea is now a cemetery.

12

Even carrion crows
sing love-songs and kiss
the lips of poets; gliding notes
as small as stones
scrawling the heart's graffiti

in the dust under your feet.

13

Perhaps
if we are lucky
we will live our way to truth
and in so doing
find the answers.

14

Life's comforts
are honeycombed
and treacherous,

and moths
appear to drink your tears
while you are sleeping.

15

A cold husband
might leave a bouquet
of dandelions on your grave
but he can't hurt you

nor mock devotion
to your scars,
your souvenirs.

Take the rest cure
then rise

and live, and go

and find a kinder lover.

16

The story goes
that swallows
with scimitars for wings
have cut your hair
and told you, you must strap it
to your horse's back
and send it home again
alone
through the forest
across snow
so white
the shadows cast are blue.

17

No.

Ariadne has a thread for you
to trace and measure
distance between the archipelagos:

Love finds a way

Look for a hole in the sky

Look.

Keep moving
and know this country — *this country*
has always belonged to you — *has always belonged to you.*

Finch

Is that you I hear singing?
Are you untangling your hair?
A finch is matching you note for note.
She has taken a place somewhere high up,
out of sight, near the eaves of your house:
the meticulous graft of long-dead bees;
a petrified eyrie – a catacomb shuttered
against the blue sky, the distant spring, against the
satisfaction of everything longed-for, rendered impossible,
but longed-for just the same.

Hold out.

There is no sign of rescue, that's for sure.
It may well be you are forgotten,
barricaded, separate. All evidence points to that,
and for all we know it might be permanent.

Know this then. Know that you still occupy
some small, forgotten corner of sweetness.
Know this – you still have light. Know this –

the finch is matching you note for note.
She is staying out the winter
somewhere high up, out of sight,
near the eaves of your house.

III

Dust

THE HEART'S GRAFFITI

The living and the dead
are gathering to listen and to judge.
The distance between them seamless

and we go on loving,
looking for gaps in the fences,
holes in the walls,
the door in the cage left open –
any way to breach frontiers,
to live slowly, deeply,
so life does not become a shorthand
for a firing-squad that kills
all the small and priceless birds
that are the gifts
of all that we are not.

Listen when a child tells you
she can see her own reflection
in your eyes. Run your fingers
over her cheek, her eyes,
her hair, and again
down the bridge of her nose
to lull her into sleeping.

The Dark

Don't be afraid of the dark.
In war the dark is on the side
of no-one but lovers.
There, they find each other.
The struggle is all over.

The future is savage,
the past beautiful,
and the map of today will be revealed
only by tomorrow.

Uncertainty is our inheritance.

Each step
makes us more lost, but that's our lot.
Don't forget what history knows.

Don't be afraid of not knowing –
decisiveness will stop
a question in its tracks.

At the Table of the World

Here, in this house,
unfinished, Spartan, roofless, concrete,
the earth has set you in its crosshairs.

Let me hold you in my gaze.

This is the table of world
and this its cloth.

Hold me.

Take each corner
in your soft, weary hands
and together we will smooth it into place –
each corner, a corner of sadness on the earth,
in need of the touch of women
at their most gentle.

Pain finds a home,
messages stuffed in pockets,
hands heavy with idleness
and the work of worry,
walls with the face of grief.

Our dead stay with us,
and swaddle us and hold us close
like fretful newborns,

and whisper softly to us in the night,
for somehow we will suffer
just a little less because of it –

despair has always a heart of some small hope.

To each, a bowl of water
in which to wash our hands,
here, salt for our wounds,
a glass from which to drink.
I will win the sunshine
through a window.

Light a candle for your table.
Bring bread.
Where is the blue sky you saw?

These napkins are prayer flags
tattered and shredded on garlands
of barbed wire. Our city is fallen,
it is stones, rubble, dust.
See here the bullets with their messages,
the prisons shattered
and reassembled in your bones.

Your ribs are window bars
that ignore the consequences,
refuse to see *what time brings –*
and now this table's cloth
is twisted like a winding sheet
around the dead.

The earth is opening its mouth
and swallowing your children
while they are gazing at the sky,
throwing stones
like insults thrown at bullets,
like wishes at stars,
like hope at hunger.

Death replies.

SILENCE

Silence makes rubble of our houses.
We are un-done.
Fact and fiction
look and smell the same.
Some drink wine and eat veal,
others must wait for the sun,
wait for the spring,
for plants to grow.

Words are too small,
far too small for history
and silence is worse than bullets,
worse than bombs,
worse than seeing and choosing unbelief.

You make your fences higher, wider, longer
and despair has looked you in the eye –
half-truths breed and multiply.

Lies are clearing the way for missiles,
and *Truth,* dressed in corsets and a scold bridle,
walks down the aisle,
showered with grim confetti
for a wedding to *Fear*.

See how the powerful live nervously.
See that what passes as a fortress,
appearing indestructible,
is braced and betrayed
by its own trembling.

It is makeshift.

History brings us messages
from the dead –

they are whispering in your ears
in the night.

Listen.

Despair

Despair is shoeless, homeless, hungry, angry.

It falls exhausted
and staggering.
It is cold, thirsty;
is poison in the water,
is hoarding,
is filth and prison, is torture,
is violence and rage,
is hatred,
is obedience,
is laws that lip-sync
making rules for silence.

It trades truth for glamour,
cowardice, hygiene, and wars
without a single body bag.
It is cold –

so cold all feeling ceases.

Indifference

Almost all promises in history are broken.
Indifference is the cruellest mutilation;
pity has no witness, no grief, no sound. No use.

Don't fear grief. Console it,
as you would a sobbing child
or one so mute with fear
it shakes the world.

Be kind.

Your house has no roof,
your road is not smooth
and you must carry the chorus in your head,
knowing the stories are passwords –
you must dream of rest and sleep out in the open,
because the powerful
fear stories most of all,
because all stories are the stories
of how the tyrants fall.

Chaos

Chaos is not some worldly untidiness,
nor just bad weather
in the same way pain
is not an accident.
No help will come from somewhere else
to save us from ourselves.

Put out the search for courage,
for wisdom, for meaning,
for we have named our children

Struggle
Sorrow
Hunger
Hatred
Tears
Blood.

In this strange world,
the dead don't have it easy –

   there are scant spoils,
   revolutions
   that leave the past to the old.

Freedom lives in humble faces
and reaches for a hand to hold,
so no one dances lonely in the night,
so that music changes time.

We want to go on living,
so no one has to grieve or suffer
or lay to waste this heart,
these bones.

This womb

will bear another revolution
and I will name it *Chaos*

for out of chaos comes a dance,

a fight for breath.

Fear

Make a cup for fear.

Collect your tears and all the cruel rain,
and, some night, when earth is at its darkest,
those days of absent moon,
put the cup out in the open
overnight, underneath the stars.

In the morning,
run your fingers across the flowers of its prayers
and drink from it –

a salve for the pain –
something for the cure.

Repeat as necessary.

Then, go on.

ACKNOWLEDGEMENTS

I would like to thank the following artists for their contribution and delivery of the Cirque des Oiseaux exhibitions, and for all of the works generated in response to these poems: Dr Simon Waters (composer) of the Sonic Arts Research Centre at Queen's University Belfast; Rosie McGurran (artist), Belfast and Connemara; Irene Uhlemann (artist), Dublin; Dr Helen Sharp (artist), Fermanagh; Bernarde Lynn (artist), Belfast; Tom Hughes (cellist and filmmaker), Belfast; Catherine Gaston (artist), Belfast; Pearl Kinnear (artist), Glasgow, and her daughter Scarlett. Thanks to Denise Griffiths and Donna Rogan at Down Arts Centre for their belief in the project and for their support in making the exhibition a reality. Thanks to Dawn Richardson (Framewerk, Belfast) and to Fermanagh and Omagh District Council, Diane Henshaw (Arts Officer) at the Higher Bridges Gallery, Enniskillen, and Denise Ferran, President of the RUA.

Thanks are also due to the poet George Szirtes for his advice and mentoring on the text; to Mary Montague; Dr Emily Murray, Ornithological Archeologist, QUB; Liam de Frinse (artist), Belfast; to Kultivera for including me in the Yeats International Residency, Tranås, Sweden (2015); to the Irish Writers Centre for a residency at Cill Rialaig Artists' Retreat in Co. Kerry; and to Poetry Ireland and the Tyrone Guthrie Centre at Annaghmakerrig, Co. Monaghan for giving me a valuable and timely inaugural bursary.

'Remnant Nomenclature' was previously published in *Abridged*; 'Faolán. Lupo. Wolf' in *The Honest Ulsterman* and on *Coracle.eu;* 'Finch' in *The Honest Ulsterman*; 'The House that Stood for Happiness' in *4 x 4 Journal*. An earlier version of 'Peregrinations' was published as 'Something for Sunday Morning' in the online journal *Poethead.* 'A Nightingale' was first published in *Washing Windows? Irish Women Write Poetry* (Arlen House, 2017).

BIBLIOGRAPHY

Attenborough, D. *New Life Stories: More Stories from his Acclaimed Radio 4 Series* (Collins, 2009).

Bachelard, G. *Air and Dreams: An Essay on the Imagination of Movement* (Dallas Institute of Humanities and Culture, 1988).

The Poetics of Space (Beacon Press, 1994).

Berger, J. *Ways of Seeing* (Penguin Books, 1972).

About Looking (Penguin Books, 1980).

Hold Everything Dear (Verso, 2016)

Bogard, P. *The End of Night: Searching for Darkness in an Age of Artificial Light* (Fourth Estate, 2013).

Bourke, E. *Piano* (Dedalus Press, 2011).

Couper, H. *The Story of Astronomy* (Cassell Illustrated, 2011).

D'Arcy, G. *Ireland's Lost Birds* (Four Courts Press, 1999).

Dee, T. *The Running Sky: A Bird-Watching Life* (Jonathan Cape, 2009).

Didion, J. *Blue Nights* (Fourth Estate, 2011).

Dorsey, M. *Perhaps the Heart is Constant After All* (Salmon Poetry, 2012).

Eno, B and Schmidt, P. *Oblique Strategies* (authors, 5th ed, 2001).

Fiennes, W. *The Snow Geese* (Random House, 2003).

GrrlScientist, 'Starlings on Prozac: How Pharmaceuticals May Affect Wildlife', http://www.theguardian.com/science/grrlscientist/2015/jul/15/starlings-on-prozac-how-pharmaceuticals-may-affect-wildlife *(published 15 July 2015).*

Harsent, D. *Night* (Faber & Faber, 2011).

Kiezer, G. *The Unwanted Sound of Everything We Want* (PublicAffairs, 2012).
Koch, L. *Memoirs of a Birdman* (Phoenix House, 1955).
Lloyd Praeger, R. *The Way that I Went* (The Collins Press, 2014).
Lawrence, E. 'Hunting the Wren', in P. Waldau and K. Patton (eds), *A Communion of Subjects: Animals in Religion, Science and Ethics* (Columbia Press, 2009).
MacDonald, H. *H is for Hawk* (Random House, 2014).
Moss, S, *Wild Hares and Hummingbirds: The Natural History of an English Village* (Vintage, 2012).
Morris, C. *Alice Milligan and the Irish Cultural Revival* (Four Courts Press, 2013).
Muldoon, P. *Birds,* after Aristophanes (Gallery Press, 1999).
Murray, E. 'Lesser Spotted Feathered Friends from Medieval Meath', *Archaeology Ireland,* 22, 3 (2008), 30–31.
Murray, E.V. 'Wolves and the Wilderness in the Middle Ages', by Aleksander Pluskowski (2006) (Circaea, 2008).
Murray, E.V. 'The Archaeology of Animal Bones' by Terry O'Connor (2000). *Antiquity* 75, (2001), 454–5.
Oddie, B. *Bill Oddie's Birds of Britain and Ireland* (New Holland, 2012).
Pretor-Pinney, G. *The Wavewatcher's Companion* (Bloomsbury, 2010).
Ridpath, I. *Collins Stars and Planets* (Collins, 2007).
Schafer, R.M. *Soundscape: Our Sonic Landscape and the Tuning of the World* (Destiny Books, 1994).
Smyth, D. *Lamentations* (Lagan Press, 2010).
Solnit, R (2001) *Wanderlust: A History of Walking* (Verso, 2001).
The Field Guide to Getting Lost (Penguin, 2006).
A Book of Migrations (Verso, 2011).
The Faraway Nearby (Granta, 2013).
Men Explain Things to Me (Haymarket, 2014).

Hope in the Dark: Untold Histories and Wild Possibilities (Haymarket Books, 2016, 3rd edition).
Stewart, I. *Earth: The Biography* (BBC, 2007).
Tudge, C. *The Secret Life of Birds* (Penguin Classics, 2008).
Webb, Jeremy, *Nothing: from Absolute Zero to Cosmic Oblivion: Amazing Insights into Nothingness (New Scientist)* (Profile Books, 2013).
Woolfson, E. *Corvus: A Life With Birds* (Granta, 2006).

About the Author

Maria is a recipient of the Artists' International Award from the Arts Council of Northern Ireland in 2016/17 as well as the inaugural 2016 Poetry Ireland/Tyrone Guthrie Centre bursary. She received an Artist's Career Enhancement (ACES) Award from the Arts Council of Northern Ireland 2015/16.

She is the author of *We are Bone* (Lagan Press, 2013), *The Cello Suites* (Lagan Press, 2009), recorded with an original score composed and played by the cellist Tom Hughes; and *Reading the Dog* (Lagan Press, 2006), her debut collection which was runner up in the 2007 Strong Awards at the Poetry Now Festival and was also shortlisted for the 2007 Glen Dimplex New Writers Award. She received the inaugural Bedell Scholarship from Aspen Writers' Foundation, USA in 2005. In 2005 she was awarded an MA with distinction from the Seamus Heaney Centre for Poetry at Queen's University Belfast. She is an experienced poetry mentor and provides mentoring through the Poetry Society, London and the Irish Writers Centre, Dublin. Her work has been translated to Polish and she has performed widely across the island of Ireland as well as in the Basque Country and at the Yeats International residency in Tranås, Sweden; Lisbon, Portugal and in Prague, Czech Republic.

In 2008 she co-wrote *Bruised* for Tinderbox Theatre Company. In 2006/07 she was playwright on attachment to Tinderbox. Previous theatre credits include *His n Her's* and *Nowhere Harder* (2006) for Replay Theatre Company; *The Black-Out Show* (2006) for Red Lead Arts and *Elizabeth Corr* for Kabosh (2016). A screenplay adaptation of the poetry sequence *Aill na Searrach : The Leap of the Foals*, was developed in 2013 with NI Screen. Other writing credits and international project work includes *The Moon. A Plane. A Crow.* which is a homage to the French *avant garde* writer Georges Perec.

Work from this collection was shortlisted for the Periplum Poetry Award of the University of Plymouth, in 2016.